know
the
game

CHESS

produced in collaboration
with the British Chess Federation

Published by A & C Black (Publishers) Ltd
35 Bedford Row, London WC1R 4JH

Contents

Foreword

Since the late fifteenth century, when the modern rules were established, chess has been the world's most popular game. The reasons for this are not hard to discern. It is extremely inexpensive to equip oneself with set and board; one can play from infancy until senility without the waning of powers that afflicts the players of more physical pursuits; luck in its conventional sense has a very slim role; the richness and variety of the game is inexhaustible; the chess player can converse through the medium of his game with the peoples of every nation; the recording of the moves makes it possible for the chess public to enjoy the games of the masters from every era as closely as if they had been present when they were played and thereby chess has the greatest and largest literature of all sports and games.

But first you must learn to play! This straightforward introduction to the game will take you to the point where you can not only play a reasonable game yourself but you can also enjoy the published games of others. Tarrasch said that 'chess, like love, like music, has the power to make men happy'. The study of this book will enable you to experience that power and if you fall within its thrall you will be the richer for it.

David Anderton
Past President and International Director
British Chess Federation

The Game

The chess beginner must first of all learn the names of the different chessmen, how they are arranged on the board, and what the object of the game is.

Chess is played on a board with sixty-four squares coloured alternately light and dark, and the board is always placed between the players so that each has a light-coloured square at his right-hand corner. The horizontal rows of squares are called *ranks* and the vertical rows are called *files*.

A chess set consists of two similar teams of sixteen *men*, one light coloured, known as White, and the other dark coloured, known as Black. In many sets, especially old ivory ones, the men are white and red, but the red men are always referred to as black.

At the start of the game the men are placed on the board as shown in Fig. 1. Notice that the White King faces Black King, White Queen faces Black Queen, etc. The player using the white men is always called 'White' and his opponent 'Black'. White always starts the game and in all diagrams White moves from the bottom of the board and Black moves from the top.

The term *man* is used to refer to any of those on the board, including the pawns, but the term *piece* refers to any of the men other than the pawns. Both players have teams as shown below:

- 8 pawns – the pawns are labelled according to the file on which they stand, e.g. a-pawn, d-pawn etc. (They might alternatively be referred to according to the piece in front of which they stand, e.g. Queen's pawn, Queen's Rook's pawn etc.)
- 2 Rooks (sometimes called Castles).
- 2 Knights.
- 2 Bishops.
- 1 Queen.
- 1 King.

Knights and Bishops are known as minor pieces and Rooks and Queens as major ones. A guide to their value (pawn = 1) is Knight or Bishop 3, Rook 5, Queen 9.

The Moves

The men can be moved on the board in various ways, but no man may move on to a square already occupied by a man of his own colour. When a man is moved to a square occupied by one of the opposing men, the latter is *taken* i.e., removed from the board and out of play.

King

The King

This is the key piece of the game because the aim is to force the opponent's King into the position where he can neither move nor remain without being taken. He is then said to be checkmated and the game is won.

The King can move in any direction, but only one square at a time, and the move must not place him in a position where he is threatened with capture by another man. He is the only man on the board which is never taken, but if he stands in such a position that he could be taken at the next move, he is said to be *in check* (see page 7).

Fig. 1

[3]

The pawns

These move one square at a time, straight up the files on which they stand. On his first move each pawn has the option of moving forward two squares but this only applies to each pawn's first move, and if he does not move up two squares on the first move he forfeits the option and cannot move two squares on a subsequent move.

Rooks or Castles

These move over as many squares as the player requires on the ranks or files, i.e. forwards, backwards or sideways. They may not be moved diagonally. The movement is limited only by the intervening presence of another man on the particular rank or file. If the man is of the same colour, i.e., friendly, the moving Rook can
[4]

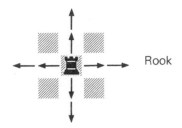

only advance as far as the square before that on which the friendly man stands. If the other man is of the opposing colour, i.e. hostile, the moving man may occupy his square and take him.

Bishops

These may be moved as far as required, but only on the diagonal, and the move is limited by the presence of other men

as in the case of Rooks. Each player has two Bishops. One starts on a white square and therefore moves diagonally on to white squares only and the other starts and moves on to black squares only.

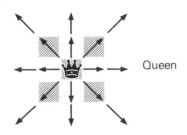

The Queen

The Queen can be moved forwards, backwards or sideways as can a Rook, and also diagonally as can a Bishop. She can, therefore, be moved as far as required in any direction, and is thus the most powerful piece on the board, owing to her greater mobility.

The move is limited by the presence of other men, as in the case of Rooks and Bishops.

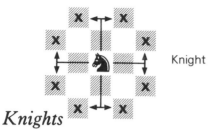

Knight

Knights

These are the only men allowed to pass over other men, whether friendly or hostile. They can be moved two squares forwards, backwards or sideways (but not diagonally), then one square at right angles to this first move. The move is only prevented by the presence of a friendly man on the final square of the required move, but not by the presence of any men on the intervening squares. A hostile man on the final square can be taken.

Thus the Queen, Rooks and Bishops have a range of movement which can be varied as the play requires, whereas the King, Knights and pawns have a fixed move. The Knights, however, cannot be blocked by the presence of other men in their path as can the others.

Special Moves

Taking procedure (pawns)

Though the pawn moves straight up, one square at a time, he may only take one square diagonally forward.

Thus in Fig. 2 the pawns block each other's path, and neither can advance further. In Fig. 2a the White pawn, having the move, can advance by

Fig. 2   Pawns block each other's path

Fig. 2a   Ringed pawn can take White pawn

taking the Black pawn shown ringed. If, in this position, the Black pawn had the move, the ringed pawn could either take the White pawn or advance one square along its own file.

Promotion of pawns

If a player succeeds in advancing a pawn to the eighth rank, i.e. on to one of the squares in the opposing first rank, it must be promoted. This is done by exchanging it for any piece except a King. When promoting a pawn no regard need be taken of the number of Queens, Rooks, Bishops or Knights already on the board. It is usual to promote the pawn to a Queen as this is the most mobile piece, and a player may then have two or more Queens on the board at the same time. The promotion takes place as part of the move which takes the pawn to the eighth rank.

Fig. 3 *En passant*. Before Black moves.

Fig. 3a *En passant*. After Black moves.

Fig. 3b White has taken *en passant*.

En Passant

When a pawn stands on his fifth rank and the opponent moves either of the two pawns on the adjacent files forward by two squares, as he has the option of doing in a pawn's first move, the pawn on the fifth rank may, on the next move only, move diagonally forward on to the square over which the opposing pawn has passed, and take that pawn. This is known as taking *en passant* or *in passing*. The move is only permissible by a pawn to a pawn, and only on the next consecutive move. Figs. 3 and 3a show the position before and after Black has moved, and Fig. 3b shows the position after White has taken en passant.

Castling

This is a special move allowed to the King, just once in a game, and is the only time a King is moved more than one square at a time. The move, which can only be made when the intervening squares between the King and Rook are not occupied, consists of moving the King two Squares to one side and then, as part of the same move, placing the Rook towards which he moves on the far side of him. This can be done provided:

1. That the squares between the King and required Rook are not occupied.
2. That neither the King nor required Rook has been moved previously during the game.
3. That the King is not in check at the time of castling, that he is not in check at the completion of castling, and that he is not in check on any square over which he passes during castling. A definition of check follows. Figs. 4 – 4c show possible positions before and after castling on each flank.

Fig. 4 Before castling

Fig. 4c After castling Queen-side

Fig. 5 Black King is in check from White Bishop.

Fig. 4a After castling King-side

Fig. 5a Check relieved by Knight taking checking Bishop.

Fig. 4b Before castling

Check

The King can never be taken, but if he stands in such a position that he is threatened with capture at the opponent's next move, he is said to be *in check*. The King must not be left in check, so a player whose King is in check must do one of three things at his next move to release him:

1. Move the King on to a square where he is out of check.
2. Take the checking piece or pawn.
3. Interpose another man so as to shield the King.

If he is unable to do any of these three things he is said to be *checkmated* and the game is ended.

Fig. 5b Check relieved by King being moved.

Fig. 5c Check relieved by interposing of Black Bishop.

In connection with point 1 above, since the King must not be moved into check, he must not be moved on to a square next to that occupied by the opposing King because he would then be in check from that piece.

In connection with point 2 above, the King may take the checking piece if it is on a square next to that on which he stands, but he must not be in check from another piece when that capture is completed.

In connection with point 3 above, if the checking piece is a Knight, it is impossible to interpose a man because the Knight would still have the King in check. In this instance, only 1 and 2 can be applied.

[8]

Figs. 6, 6a and 6b show three simple positions of checkmate, but there is obviously an infinite variety of checkmating positions.

In Fig. 6, although the King can move one square in any direction he will still be in check by the Rook on the eighth rank if he moves on to square **a** or **e**, and by the Rook on the seventh rank if he moves on to square **b, c** or **d**.

In Fig. 6a, the Black King is in check by the Queen and will still be in check by the Queen if he moves to square **a, b, c** or **d**. It is not permissible to take the Queen because she is protected by the White King.

In Fig. 6b the Black King is still in check by the Rook if he moves to squares **a** or **e**, and he cannot move to squares **b, c** or **d** because of the White King.

Fig. 6c shows a special variety of checkmate known as a *smothered* mate since the escape of the Black King is impeded, not by the White pieces, but by his own men. He is in check by the White Knight which can pass over the intervening Black Bishop and Queen.

Fig. 6

Fig. 6a

Fig. 6b

Fig. 6c

Thus it will be seen that the completion of a game of chess is not dependent on the number of pieces taken, but on the attainment of a position of checkmate. However, a superiority of pieces usually makes a victory more certain in the long run.

Other Game Endings

A game does not always end with a checkmate and a player whose chances of escaping defeat are clearly hopeless may avoid waste of time by *resigning*, i.e. conceding the game to his opponent.

In addition, a game can end in a draw, as follows:

1. Both players agree to a draw since they know from experience that the position is of such tactical equality that a win cannot be obtained.
2. When the pieces have been eliminated to a point where checkmate is no longer possible, agreement to draw is advised.
   Figs. 7, 7a, 7b and 7c show positions when it is futile to continue in the hope of a win.

Note: It is possible to force a win against a King with a King and two Bishops or a King, Knight and Bishop, but not with a King and two Knights (unless the opponent plays incorrectly).

Fig. 7

Fig. 7a

Fig. 7b

Fig. 7c

Fig. 8

Fig. 8a

Fig. 8b

3. Another form of drawn position is that known as a *stalemate*, i.e. when the opposing King is not in check but the opponent is unable to make any legal move either with his King or any other man. Figs. 8 and 8a show two examples of a stalemate.

4. The game is drawn if a player can show that 50 consecutive moves have been made without a man being taken or a pawn moved (100 moves in a small number of specified positions).

5. Another type of draw is a draw by *perpetual check*, when one player can show that he can submit his opponent to an endless series of checks.

6. A game can be drawn if one player can show that exactly the same position has recurred three times during the game. The most usual example of this type of draw is when the same move is made three times consecutively.

In Fig. 8b Black has a winning advantage of material (i.e., a Rook to the good) and threatens checkmate, but White has the move and is able to force perpetual check.

Fig. 8c with Black to move shows an actual finish of an international game. In this, it is interesting to note that Black can afford to offer his Rook, a piece which White dare not take for fear of being mated two moves later.

In both examples therefore, it is clear that the check can continue for ever. In the unlikely event of the

Fig. 8c

opponent refusing to admit that the check is perpetual a draw can be obtained after the third repetition of a similar position.

Solution (Fig. 8c)

1. ...   Rg1+
2. Kh2   Rh1+

If 3. K×h1 Qb1+   and mate follows, but if 3. Kg2 or g3, then draw by repetition.

Rules of Play

Before the beginner starts his first game he must learn some of the more important rules of play. The following is not by any means a list of all the rules, but the essential points for a beginner are covered.

1. A move consists of picking up a man and transferring it to another square. The move is not completed until the player has removed his hand from the man he is moving.
2. A man that has been touched must be moved. If the player changes his mind about the move before completing it he may make an alternative move, but it must be with the man already touched.
3. If a player touches one or more pieces of the same colour he must move or capture the first piece touched that can be moved or captured.
4. If a player touches one of his own pieces and one of his opponent's pieces, he must capture his opponent's piece with his own piece; or, if this is not possible, move his own piece; or if this is not possible, capture his opponent's piece.
5. Once a move has been completed it cannot be retracted.
6. A player may at any time arrange his men on the board but he must tell his opponent before he does so. He may also ask his opponent to arrange his own men but he must not touch or arrange his opponent's men.
7. If an illegal move is made and discovered later in the game, the men must be set out in the positions they occupied before the illegal move and the game restarted with a legal move using the man used for the illegal move. If the positions before the illegal move cannot be decided, the game must be discontinued and is void.
8. If a penalty cannot legally be complied with, a further penalty is not enforced.

9. The players must not comment on any moves while the game is in progress, nor may they consult any written notes which bear upon the game being played or analyse it on another chessboard during playing sessions.

10. Players are forbidden to distract or annoy their opponents in any manner whatsoever.

11. Players must not seek advice or information from onlookers while the game is in progress. Spectators should refrain from commenting on games in progress.

Notation

The beginner is now ready to start playing in earnest and he will need some guidance on elementary tactics and strategy. Reference will have to be made to particular moves on the board so it is necessary to understand how chess moves are recorded on paper.

There are two main systems of notation and these are the *Algebraic system* and the *Descriptive system*.

The Algebraic System

This is now the only system recognized by the World Chess Federation for games played in its own tournaments and matches.

1. Each piece is indicated by the first (capital) letter of its name,
   K = king, Q = queen, R = rook,
   B = bishop and N is used for knight. In printed publications the use of figurines is recommended, especially on diagrams.

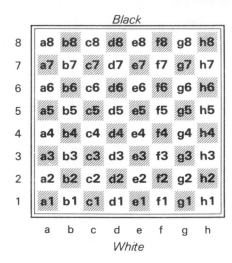

Fig. 9 Algebraic Notation

2. Pawns are not indicated by their first letter, but pawn moves are recognized by the absence of such a letter. E.g. e3, d4, a5.

3. The eight files (from left to right for White and from right to left for Black) are indicated by the small letters a, b, c, d, e, f, g, and h respectively.

4. The eight ranks are numbered 1 to 8, always from White's end. Consequently, in the initial position the White pieces and pawns are placed on the first and second ranks; the Black pieces and pawns on the eighth and seventh ranks.

5. As a consequence of the previous rules, each of the sixty four squares is invariably indicated by a unique combination of a letter and a number (see Fig. 9).

6. Each move of a piece is indicated by the first letter of the piece in question and by the square of arrival. There is no hyphen between the two. E.g. Be5, Nf3, Rdl. In the case of pawns, only the square of arrival is indicated. E.g. e3, d4, a5.

7. When a piece makes a capture an × is inserted between the first letter of the piece in question and the square of arrival. E.g. B×e5, N×f3, R×dl. When a pawn makes a capture, not only the square of arrival but also the file of departure must be indicated, with an × in between. E.g. d×e3, g×f3, a×b5. In the case of an *en passant* capture the square of arrival is given as the square on which the capturing pawn finally rests and 'e.p.' is appended to the notation.

8. If two identical pieces can move to the same square, the piece that is moved is indicated as follows:
   (i) If both pieces are on the same rank:
       by (a) the first letter of the name of the piece, (b) the file of departure and (c) the square of arrival.
   (ii) If both pieces are on the same file:
       by (a) the first letter of the name of the piece, (b) the number of the square of departure, and (c) the square of arrival.
   (iii) If the pieces are on different ranks and files, method (i) is preferred.
   In case of a capture, an × must be inserted between (b) and (c).

Examples
1. There are two Knights, on squares c4 and f3, and one of them moves to square e5; either Nce5 or Nfe5, as the case may be.
2. There are two Knights, on squares g5 and g1, and one of them moves to square f3; either N5f3 or N1f3, as the case may be.
3. There are two Knights, on squares h2 and d4, and one of them moves to square f3; either Nhf3 or Ndf3, as the case may be.

If a capture takes place on square e5, example 1. is changed by the insertion of an ×: Nc×e5 or Nf×e5 (see Fig. 11).

9. See Fig. 11a. If two pawns can capture the same piece or pawn of the opponent, the pawn that is moved is indicated by the letter of the file of departure, an × and the square of arrival. E.g. if there are white pawns on the squares c4 and e4 and a black pawn or piece on the

square d5, the notation for White's move is either c×d5 or e×d5, as the case may be.

10. In the case of the promotion of a pawn, the actual pawn move is indicated, followed immediately by the first letter of the new piece. E.g. d8Q, f8N, b1B, g1R.

Essential abbreviations

O–O	castling with Rook h1 or Rook h8 (King-side castling)
O–O–O	castling with Rook a1 or Rook a8 (Queen-side castling)
×	captures
+	check
++	mate
e.p.	captures *en passant*

Sample Game

1. d4, Nf6;	2. c4, e6;	3. Nc3, Bb4;
4. Bd2, 0.0;	5. e4, d5;	6. e×d5, e×d5;
7. c×d5, B×c3;	8. B×c3,N×d5;	9. Nf3, b6;
10. Qb3, N×c3;	11. b×c3, c5;	12. Be2, c×d4;
13. N×d4, Re8;	14. O–O, Nd7;	15. a4, Nc5;
16. Qb4, Bb7;	17. a5, b×a5. etc.	

The Descriptive System

Although the Descriptive system is much more cumbersome than the Continental system, it is still used in many British books and articles on chess.

The Bishops, Knights and Rooks on the King's side are known as King's Bishop, King's Knight and King's Rook and those on the Queen's side are known as Queen's Bishop, Queen's Knight and Queen's Rook.

The files are known by the name of the pieces standing on them at the start of the game.

The squares are numbered 1 — 8 along the files from each end, and each square is referred to by the file name and square number, e.g., King's Bishop 1.

It will be seen that White King's Bishop 1 is the same as Black King's Bishop 8, etc. and Fig. 10a shows the board with the square names marked in white to indicate the White viewpoint and black to represent Black.

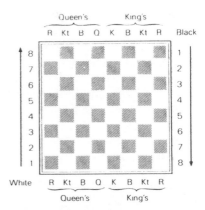

Fig. 10 Descriptive Notation.

The pawns are known by the names of their files, i.e., King's Rook's pawn, or Queen's Knight's pawn, etc.

The standard abbreviations are:

K	King
Q	Queen
P	Pawn
KB	King's Bishop
QB	Queen's Bishop
K Kt (or KN)	King's Knight
Q Kt (or QN)	Queen's Knight

Fig. 10a Descriptive Notation

It will be clearly seen from Figs. 9, 10 and 10a how the different squares are named for the purpose of recording the various moves.

If White, as his first move, advances his King's pawn by two squares, the notation is 1. P — K4, indicating that the pawn on the King's file has been advanced to the fourth rank. If Black replies by a similar advance of his King's pawn it is recorded 1. P — K4. If then White advances his King's Knight two squares up the file and one square at right angles on to the Bishop's file the notation is 2. Kt — KB3 (correct also is KKt — B3), and if Black protects his now menaced King's pawn by a similar movement of his Queen's Knight the record is 2. Kt. — QB3 (or QKt — B3).

The complete record would read:
1. P — K4, P — K4
2. Kt — KB3, Kt — QB3

In descriptive notation the piece taken is shown, not the square on which the capture occurred, e.g. B×B means Bishop takes Bishop.

Castling is indicated by O—O or O—O—O and a piece taken by × as in algebraic notation. Check is indicated by ch.

If more than one similar piece can make the required move the record must clearly show which one is to be moved.

Thus in Fig. 11 it can be seen that either Knight can take the Black Bishop, and the record would read Kt (B3) × B, or Kt (B4) × B according to which Knight has to make the capture.

Fig. 11 Record must indicate which Knight takes the Black Bishop

Fig. 11a c×d5 or e×d5
(KP×P or BP×P)

Fig. 11b B×P

Similarly in Fig. 11a the move to take the Black pawn must be recorded KP × P or BP × P, according to which pawn makes the capture.

Fig. 11b shows a well-known position of the men on the board. The White Bishop has the choice of taking one of two Black pawns. It is not necessary to indicate which of two pawns is to be taken, because the record B × P refers only to the Black Bishop's pawn; if the Rook's pawn is to be taken, the record would be B × P ch., since the Black King would be in check when the move was completed. [16]

General Strategy

The beginner is now able to set out his board and men, knows the permissible moves, can record those moves, and has a knowledge of the basic rules of the game and its object. Next he can consider some of the principles of elementary strategy and tactics.

A game of chess should always be governed by a definite scheme, or series of schemes, all moving in accordance with a general strategical plan but modified from time to time to meet immediate tactical necessities. With inexperienced players the general scheme may be somewhat hazy, and therefore the game will develop more or less accidentally from a series of problems and tactical threats dealt with move by move.

This need not worry the beginner because every game he plays will widen his experience (especially if he plays against a stronger opponent) until he has gained a reasonable grasp of general tactics. Each move should have an intended purpose. A move may be wrong because the reason is wrong, but practice, tuition and experience will correct the reasoning in due course. Aimless chess is invariably bad chess and losing chess.

The aim of every player is to checkmate his opponent, but since the players start the game each with the same number of men in opposing positions, it is obvious that several moves must be made before a direct attack can be attempted on the hostile

King. It is necessary therefore for the beginner to concentrate first on gaining positional advantages which may lead to material ones at a later stage.

The basic strategical principle generally adopted is to try to gain control of the centre, i.e., of the squares e4, e5, d4, and d5 (K4, K5, Q4, and Q5) and those adjacent to them. If such a control can be successfully established a winning continuation will usually be forthcoming provided that the player can find it. Players should seek to gain advantages by using pieces and pawns in conjunction with each other, trying to develop a purposeful attack but not overlooking the need to thwart an opponent's attack. Concentration on one flank tends to have the disadvantage that the opponent will probably take counter-measures on the opposite flank. Often one player is attacking on one flank while the other is launching a counter-attack on the other side with neither bothering to concentrate on defensive measures at the threatened spot, and the victory goes to the player whose attack gets home first.

Control is a word frequently used when describing chess tactics. A square is said to be controlled by a player when he has more pieces bearing on it than his opponent has. Therefore a square need not be occupied to be controlled, and, in fact, even if a square is occupied it is not controlled unless the occupying man is adequately defended by at least as many men as there are hostile men attacking it.

From this definition it can be seen that there are two methods of attaining central control, the first by advancing pawns into the centre and maintaining them by adequate support, and the second by reserving an initial pawn advance by bringing the longer-ranged pieces such as the Knights and Bishops to bear on the centre squares from a distance. In this second case an eventual central pawn advance will have to be made but the strategical idea is that, whereas an immediate advance commits a player to a definite course of action, the reservation of such an advance leaves the opponent without such a clear-cut tactical problem for solution.

In practice, however, it is usually found that White prefers to exploit his advantage of the first move by an immediate pawn advance into the centre. In former years Black invariably met such an advance with a similar reply so as to maintain a 50% control of the centre by symmetry of moves, but today the reservation of the central pawn advance is also frequently used. Thus the move 1. d4 is often met by 1. ... Nf6 and 1. e4, by 1. ... c5, in each case contesting the advance of a second pawn in the centre by White but reserving the advance of either of the Black central pawns.

Opening Moves

Having considered the basic strategical ideas of the start of a chess game, we must now consider the immediate tactical problems likely to be met in trying to put them into effect. If both players rush aimlessly into the centre, there will be some sort of general exchange leading to an eventual draw. It is therefore necessary to manoeuvre with a view to making moves which will leave the opponent's pieces in bad positions, or possibly to offer the sacrifice of a pawn or even a piece in order to obtain a better position if the sacrifice is accepted.

For example, one well known move which achieves this is called the *Greek Bishop*. In this series of moves, the Bishop is placed so it can take the h-pawn while at the same time there is no opposing Knight on f6. In Fig. 12 play with White to move would go:
1. B×h7+, K×h7
2. Ng5+, Kg8
3. Qh5
and wins since Black has no adequate

[18]

Fig. 12   Greek Bishop

defence against the threat of the fourth move Qh7++. It is, of course, open to Black to decline the sacrifice by playing 1. ... Kh8, but if he does he will lose a pawn and his King will be dangerously exposed. He can also play 2. ... Kg6, but then his King will not escape disaster for more than a few moves in such an open unprotected position.

Pawn sacrifices can occur at any time in the game, but they are most frequently found early on in the game in a gambit theme. In this a pawn,

known as the *gambit pawn*, is sacrificed with the idea thereby of decreasing the opponent's ability to fight for the control of the central squares.

The gambit pawn is usually on one of the Bishop's files so that, if the offer is accepted, one of the opposing pawns is drawn off the central files. If the gambit is offered in the opening stages it is known as the *King's Gambit* or the *Queen's Gambit*, according to whether the f or c pawn is sacrificed.
The opening moves of the King's and Queen's gambits respectively are:

1. e4, e5   1. d4, d5
2. f4   and   2. c4

as shown in Figs. 13 and 13a.

In the Victorian and Edwardian eras the King's Gambit attacks proved very dangerous and led to some extremely brilliant games, owing to the fact that Black invariably tried to hold his pawn advantage. For this reason it later became more customary for players to decline gambits when offered. Modern analysis, however, has shown that the correct treatment of gambits is to accept the gambit pawn and then to

Fig. 13 King's Gambit

Fig. 13a Queen's Gambit

concentrate on reaching positional equality without trying to hold the extra pawn. If this course is followed Black can achieve equality of position with little trouble, and to such an extent has this proved to be the case that gambit openings, with the exception of the Queen's Gambit, are rarely found in first-class chess today because they offer too safe a drawing chance to the second player.

The **Queen's Gambit** can be accepted or declined with equal success provided that Black plays his game accurately, but it is being played less today because the answer to 1. d4 is far more often 1. ... Nf6 than 1. ... d5, following the theory of a delayed central pawn advance. In such cases it is not possible to offer the c-pawn as a gambit.

In gambits based on the opening

1. e4 the basic principles for Black are:
1. To accept the gambit pawn.
2. To concentrate on a development which combats the control of the centre, and to return the gambit pawn in the course of play, unless White by incorrect moves allows him to retain his pawn advantage safely.
3. To play . . . d5 successfully as soon as possible.

Once Black has achieved the last-named objective, he has gained equality of position, but it must be emphasised that he must be able to play . . . d5 *successfully*. To play this move in the face of an already established control is merely suicidal.

Typical opening moves against the **King's Gambit** used to be:

1. e4, e5
2. f4, e × f4
3. Nf3, g5

Here Black is trying to hold his pawn advantage, and it is against such attempts that this opening can be so dangerous. The more modern continuation would probably be:

[19]

1. e5, e5
2. f4, e×f4
3. Nf3, d5
4. e×d5, Nf6

Here Black has returned the gambit pawn and successfully played . . . d5 with the result that, although he no longer has a pawn advantage, he has no disadvantage of position. In this example it would be incorrect for White to play 4. e5 because Black could then reply 4. . . . g5 and hold his pawn advantage. This is the type of positional mistake referred to in 2. on page 19. If in the above line of play White plays 3. Bc4 play could go:

3. . . . d5
4. B×d5, Nf6
5. Nc3, Bb4

Finally it may be mentioned that the attractive-looking move 3. . . . Qh4+ leads to no advantage for Black, whose Queen remains open to attack, while the White King's loss of castling rights is only a minor inconvenience.

In the opening known as the **Danish Gambit**, Black's three basic principles expressed in the following moves can

[20]

be successfully applied:

1. e4, e5
2. d4, e×d4
3. c3, d5
4. e×d5, Q×d5
5. c×d4, Nc6
6. Nf3, Nf6
7. Nc3, Bb4

reaching the position shown in Fig. 14. Here again Black has successfully played . . . d5 at move 3, and in the ensuing pawn exchanges has returned the gambit pawn but gained a solid equality of position.

Fig. 14

Notice that Black's last move protects his Queen by *pinning* the White Knight which cannot move without disclosing a check. Such pins play a great part in the tactics of chess.

Against openings 1. e4, e5 the struggle for central control is usually decided by whether or not Black can force the move . . . d5 successfully, and this applies equally to lines of play where no gambits are employed.

The examples just given of gambit play illustrate the need to plan the opening of a game of chess. Both sides try to develop their pieces as quickly as possible within the guiding limits of the strategy they have in mind.

As an alternative to gambit play some chess players have changed to lines leading to restriction of hostile development, and in such lines there are many pawn moves which can be most useful. It may be thought that this idea of restriction is defensive rather than offensive and consequently undesirable, but this is not always so. Strength in the opening stages will always be equal over the whole board, but not necessarily so in any one part of it, and these local discrepancies play a big part in the making of plans for attack or defence.

During the present century, chess theory and analysis have reached a high level of intensity and it is growing more and more difficult to win by the comparatively simple and direct means employed by former generations. With the advent of computer technology beginners can gain experience from analysing their own play in their own homes. Most computers play openings accurately and the quality of play over the first ten or twelve moves has improved rapidly in recent years. The tendency is now rather to aim at reaching positional advantages which restrict the opponent's freedom of movement by denying him the use of certain squares. In such games pawns are of paramount importance. The offensive idea still remains as in the case of a boxer who tries to manoeuvre his opponent into a corner of the ring before going into attack.

The Middle Game

We have considered the principles of opening play and now we must consider those underlying the game in its next stages, known as the middle game. The struggle for central control may have been settled one way or the other and the players will be making further plans for gaining the final objective of the game, the checkmating of the opponent.

At this stage both players will be mainly concerned with the gaining and the prevention of tactical or positional advantages. Faulty play in the opening by one of the players could present a weakness of position ready-made for exploitation, and therefore an early result.

Accurate planning is essential for success, and a constant search should be maintained to discover small positional advantages and also to avoid similar chances for the opponent in the player's own position. To do this, the player must learn to correctly appreciate the existing situation in the same ways as a General studies military tactics. Positions, strength, mobility, and objectives must be considered and a plan formed by which it is hoped to win the game.

Each player should try to understand his opponent's objective as indicated by his moves but if, after due consideration, no real reason appears to underlie a specific move by the opponent then the player should ignore it and continue with his own plans. Unrecognised, and possibly non-existent, dangers should never be allowed to deter a chess player. If there is a threat which has not been realised the player will soon learn it and his experience will be enlarged thereby.

A direct attack on the opposing King will not often be possible in the early stages of the middle game, but if any small weakness of position can be found in the hostile ranks, and can be successfully exploited, then the attacker can often gain ultimate victory as a result. Thus, however attractive it may be to make direct attacks towards the hostile King, it is usually sounder

[21]

strategy to locate a positional weakness, often in another part of the board, and to concentrate all available forces on exploiting it.

The most frequent weaknesses in positions occur in the pawn formations, largely because a pawn cannot retreat and therefore, when once moved, is committed for better or worse. The most common weakness among the pawns is what is known as a *backward pawn*.

A backward pawn is one which stands on a file on which there is no hostile pawn and which cannot be defended by one of its own pawns. Such a pawn should be attacked at once with all forces possible. If it can be won, a winning position can usually be gained out of the ensuing exchanges, while if not, then at least the opponent will be compelled to tie up most of his forces in defending it.

There are other weaknesses such as a piece left unprotected or a piece pinned down, but these are normally temporary, while a pawn weakness is usually of a fixed and lasting type, and, [22]

if properly exploited by the opponent, is most troublesome and even dangerous. Options open to the player with a backward pawn are:

1. To defend it as well as possible.
2. To force it forward to a point where it is defended by another pawn and so is no longer backward.
3. To force the pawn forward so as to get rid of it by exchange.
4. To block the file with a piece and so protect the pawn from attack.
5. To force an exchange which will compel the opponent to retake on to the file with a pawn, then the pawn will no longer be backward.
6. To abandon the pawn to its fate but to try to gain a pawn somewhere else on the board in exchange, or at any rate some compensating positional advantage.

Fig. 15 shows a Black d-pawn which is both isolated and backward. White has concentrated his attack on it and is now about to take it. He is attacking it with a Queen, two Rooks, a Knight and a Bishop, a total of five pieces, against Black's defending

Fig. 15

Queen, Rook, Knight and Bishop, a total of four pieces.

Sometimes, however, it is not necessary to win a backward pawn to win a game, because the threat to the pawn may lead the opponent to adopt a losing line to try to save it. In the position shown in Fig. 16 Black had an ingenious plan for liquidating his backward c-pawn which, however, led to a loss because it left his Queen in a weak position.

Fig. 16

Play after White's 16th move went as follows:

16.		B×e4
17.	Q×e4	c5
18.	d×c5	Qa5(a)
19.	b3(b)	B×c5
20.	Ng5	h6(c)
21.	Qh7+	Kf8
22.	Qh8+	Ke7
23.	Q×g7	h×g5
24.	Q×g5+	Kd6
25.	Ke2	Rac8
26.	Rc4(d)	Kc6
27.	Rhc1	Kb6(e)
28.	h4(f)	f5(g)
29.	Qg7	Re7
30.	Qe5	Rc6
31.	R×c5(h)	Resigns

(See below for an explanation of the letters in brackets after moves 18, 19, 20, 26, 27, 28.)

(a) The plan matures, but Black has in the process moved his Queen out of the game.

(b) White cannot give up his a-pawn because of Black's subsequent deadly wing pawn attack.

(c) Black thinks he can get his King to safety on the Queen's wing if White attacks, and such an attack must cost White his Knight. White, however, is prepared to sacrifice.

(d) Preparing 27. Rd1+. Black sees this and moves before he is driven.

(e) The Black Queen now has no move.

(f) White h-pawn can now advance unopposed.

(g) Another defence would be 28. ... Rc7; then White should still win by

29. h5, Rec8; 30. h6, Bd6; 31. Q×a5+, K×a5; 32. R×c7, B×c7; (if 32. ... R×c7; 33. h7!) 33. Rc6! etc.

(h) Answering 31. ... R×c5 by 32. Qd6+ etc.

Another example of weakness in a formation is that of *holes* or *outposts* which may be occupied successfully by an opposing piece. The definition of an outpost is that it should be a square which cannot be attacked by an opposing pawn.

Outposts are most commonly created on the fifth rank by the advance of the opposing pawns to their fourth rank. Fig. 17 shows an ideal outpost at c5, where the White Knight cannot even be exchanged off for the opposing minor piece.

It will be noted that White has an alternative outpost on e5.

Fig. 17

Fig. 18

As a general rule it is most profitable to occupy an available outpost with a Knight, and there are occasions when it will be sound play to accept a losing exchange, i.e., to give up a Rook for a minor piece in order to get a Knight on to the required square.

Fig. 18 gives an example of such play, and it will be noted how the White Knight, once established, hampers the Black defence at every turn and finally supports a winning attack.

[24]

	White	Black
1.	R×e6	f×e6
2.	Ng4	Kg7
3.	Qf3	Rf8
4.	Nf6(a)	Qc6
5.	h4	Ra7
6.	Rf1	Qc8
7.	Qg4(b)	Nf5(c)
8.	Rf3	Raf7(d)
9.	Q¾g6+(e)	Kh8
10.	B×f5	Resigns(f)

(a) Now the Knight stands firm on his outpost, dominating all Black's efforts.

(b) Threatening 8. B×g6, N×g6; 9. h5 winning.

(c) An effort to shut out the threat of the White Bishop and to bring his a. Rook into action.

(d) This move, which seems to get Black out of trouble, is actually suicide.

(e) If 9 … K×g6, Rg3++

(f) There is no reply to Q×h6+

Another common weakness in the pawn formation is made by the movement of the pawns in front of a castled King. Although such moves sometimes have to be made, they should never be made unless absolutely forced since a potential weakness is always left which the opponent may be able to exploit later in the game, if not immediately (as in the previous example).

Fig. 19 shows a position in which Black has played … h6 at some earlier stage in the game, and in subsequent play White has manoeuvred to be able to

Fig. 19

Fig. 20

1.	...	h6
2.	N×f7	R×f7
3.	Qg6	Qd7
4.	Rf3	Nd5(a)
5.	R×f7	Q×f7
6.	Re8+	Resigns

(a) If 4. ... Kf8; 5. R×f6, R×f6;
6. Qh7 and wins or if 5. ... g×f6;
6. Q×h6+, Kg8; 7. Re3 and wins.
Once again it will be seen that the pin
by the White Bishop played a great part
in these manoeuvres.

sacrifice a Rook, thereby gaining a winning attack.

Play, after Black's 22nd move, went as follows:

23.	R×h6	g×h6
24.	Qg6+	Kh8
25.	Q×h6+	Kg8
26.	Rd5	

and won since Black could not defend the threat of checkmate by 27. Rg5.

Notice that after 24. Qg6+ Black could not play 24. ... f×g6 because this move would disclose a check from the White Bishop on c4. In other words the pawn was pinned, another example of the value and danger of such pins.

In Fig. 20 Black moved a pawn in front of his castled King, although he was not forced to do so by his opponent. He made this move out of fear of attack from the White Knight which he wished to drive away. The results of failure to defend accurately were disastrous:

The Endgame

After the above brief examples of tactical ideas in the middle game, we examine some general principles of endgame play. This part of the game is of the greatest importance, since it is possible for a good endgame player to retrieve a disadvantageous middle game, or for a good middle game to be thrown away by poor endgame play.

All players are strongly recommended to play out their games as often as possible to a point where a decisive position is reached. For novices, it is excellent practice for all games to be played right out to a checkmate without any resignations.

The field of endgame play is so vast that it is only possible to give a very brief outline of some of the more common basic types, but these will establish certain principles which can be applied to endgames in general.

It has already been stated that checkmate is possible against a solitary King by King and Queen, King and

[26]

Fig. 21 Winning position for King and two Bishops.

Fig. 21a Winning position for King, Bishop and Knight.

Rook, King and two Bishops, and King, Bishop and Knight.

Figs. 7, 7a and 7b have shown the checkmating position with King and Rook.

It will be seen that the play in each case is to drive the opposing King into a corner. In the case of King, Bishop and Knight, it must be a corner square of the same colour as that on which the Bishop stands. He is then pinned there with the King and Bishop restricting

his move to the Rooks' and Knights' squares. After this the third piece is brought up to co-operate in the mate. Such endgames are, however, of mainly theoretical interest as they are rarely likely to occur in actual play.

As a general rule, most endgames tend to centre round the struggle to win by the promotion of a pawn, and they can be classed generally under the following headings:

(a) King and pawn against King.

(b) King and pawn against King and piece.

(c) King, Rook and pawn endings.

Before considering endgames in detail it is necessary to define three terms frequently used:

1. The Square (sometimes known as Cordon).
2. The opposition.
3. Self-supporting pawns.

The Square

This is an imaginary square on the board. One side is made up of the square on which the pawn stands and the squares up to and including its eighth rank. The Black outline in Fig. 22 shows the square of the pawn on g3, and the dotted line shows its square after it has advanced one square to g4.

The opposing King, in order to catch the pawn before it can achieve

promotion, must be able to enter the square before the pawn moves. In Fig. 22 Black can do this if he has the move, but if White moves first then the pawn will enter the smaller square and cannot be caught in time.

The Opposition

A King is said to have the opposition when he is separated from the other King by an odd number of squares either on a file, rank or diagonal, and the opposing King has the move. In Fig. 23 the White King has the opposition if it is Black's turn to move, and the dotted squares indicate the other squares on the board on which the Black King could stand and the Kings still be in opposition. The gaining or avoidance of the opposition is the most important individual tactical feature of endgame play.

The tactical value of having the opposition is that the opposing King is forced to concede control of squares to his opponent when he moves, and that

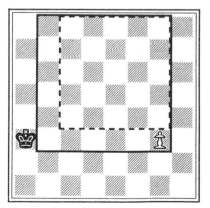

Fig. 22 The Square

[27]

Fig. 23

Fig. 24

Black pawns. The example is a simple one which the novice can work out for himself.

the latter then has the choice of moving so as to keep the opposition or of taking advantage of the territory conceded.

In the former case he would be playing for a draw, and in the latter for a win. In Fig. 24 Black can draw if he has the opposition, since he will be able to keep the opposition after each move, but if White has the opposition, i.e. Black has to move first, then White must be able to win by taking one of the

Self-supporting pawns

Pawns are so described when they are in a position where they cannot be attacked by the hostile King and one of them taken without the other one being able to reach the eighth rank and gain promotion. In Fig. 25 both sets of pawns are self-supporting. The case of the White pawns is clear since if Black plays 1. ...K×b4, White answers 2. a6 and the Black King cannot catch it as he is outside the square. The Black pawns, however, require more careful play, and the rule is that the pawns should not be moved until one of them is attacked, and then the other one should be moved. Thus play might go:

1. Ke6   h5 (moving the unattacked pawn)
2. Kf5   Ka6
3. Kf4   Kb5
4. Kg3   f5
5. Kh4   f4, etc.

Fig. 25

Fig. 26

Fig. 27

King and pawn against King

In endings where a King and pawn face a King alone a win should only be gained if the King can lead his pawn on the sixth rank. If this position can be reached the pawn can be forced home whether its King has the opposition or not. The term 'should' is used because it is always possible for a player to throw away a won or drawn position by incorrect play. In Fig. 26 White can only win if he has the move.

1.	Kd2	Kd7		1.	...	Ke7
2.	Kd3	Ke7	but	2.	Kd2	Ke6
3.	Ke4	Ke6		3.	Ke3	Ke5
4.	e3 and wins				securing the opposition and drawing.

Note: in the first example White can only win because he has the waiting move 4. e3 at his disposal. If the pawn had started on K3 the game would have been drawn as Black would have the opposition.

Fig.27 provides an interesting study of the necessity for really careful calculation of time and distance. Play went:

1.	b5+	Kb7
2.	a6+	Kb6
3.	Kb4	Kc7

and a draw was agreed because White was afraid to take his King up the board to force one of his pawns through

[29]

as this would leave the Black d-pawn free to advance. It was, however, possible for White to win despite the promotion of the Black pawn, e.g.:

4.	Kc5	d3
5.	b6+	Kb8
6.	Kc6	d2
7.	a7+	Ka8
8.	Kc7	d1Q
9.	b7+	K×a7
10.	b8Q+	Ka6
11.	Qb6++	

Thus it will be seen that these King and pawn endings offer many possibilities for error and need careful calculation and play. The main tactical points for consideration are:

1. The calculation of distances, e.g. the square.
2. The correct evaluation of the need to gain or avoid the opposition.
3. The tactical implications of passed or self-supporting pawns.

Note: A *passed pawn* is one which can advance without interference from another hostile pawn.

When there are two pawns against one, having the opposition is of great

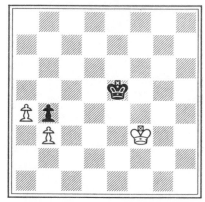

Fig. 28

value. In Fig. 28 Black cannot win since the White pawns are self-supporting and so cannot be attacked without one being able to reach the eighth rank. Black must, therefore, play for a draw which he can get if he has the move but not otherwise:

1. ... Kd5
2. Kf4 Kd4 or 2. Ke3 Ke5

and Black draws by keeping the opposition indefinitely. With the move, White wins by:

1. Ke3 Kd5
2. Kd3 Kc5
3. Ke4 Kc6
4. Kd4 and wins.

Note: It does not matter if Black plays 3 ... Kb6 or Kc6. It should also be noted that White cannot win by an immediate advance of the a-pawn since the Black King is within its square and so can catch it, after which Black can get a draw on the lines shown in Fig. 26.

The final assessment of an endgame position depends as much on position as on number of men left. Equality of men normally means a draw, and superiority such as an extra pawn should usually enable a win to be obtained. One of the most common positions where equality does not mean a draw is that in which there is a distant passed pawn. This is a pawn which stands on the far side of the board from the main body of pawns, so that the opposing King cannot stop it queening, and at the same time protect

Fig. 29

his own pawns from attack by the other King.

In Fig. 29 it will be seen that after:

1. g4   f×g4
2. h×g4

the White g-pawn is passed and distant, so that if the Black King opposes its advance the White King can win the Black pawns and can then force a Queen on the Queen's side of the board. If the Black King goes to the defence of his own pawns, the distant g-pawn queens unopposed.

King and pawn against King and piece

In the King and pawn against King and piece ending, the game is usually a draw if the piece is a minor one. This is because it is not possible to force checkmate with a King and minor piece, and so the player with the piece merely gives it up for the pawn, leaving two Kings only on the board and a drawn game. Only in very exceptional circumstances is it possible to avoid such a sacrifice. It may be occasionally possible to queen the pawn and win if the Knight or Bishop is hopelessly misplaced.

With regard to major pieces, the result of a King and pawn against King and Rook depends entirely on the position. It is clear that the pawn must be taken without the loss of the Rook, and the Rook alone cannot stop the advance of the King and pawn. Thus the result usually depends on the positions of the Kings.

If the pawn is well forward and closely supported by its King, the game can often be drawn, but if the opposing King is already in front of it the game is always lost. It is impossible to lay down a rule for such positions and each must be judged on its merits. But it can be said that a King and Rook will not necessarily win against a King and pawn.

The only other major piece is the Queen, and here the position is more definite. A King and Queen can win against a King and pawn except when the pawn has reached the seventh rank on a Bishop's or Rook's file and is supported by its King. In such a position, unless the opposing King is close to the pawn, the King and pawn can draw. The principle of the win with the King and Queen is to check the King until he is driven in front of his pawn and then to take advantage of the blocking of the pawn to advance the Queen's King towards the pawn. These tactics are repeated until the King is next to the pawn and the Queen can take it without being retaken.

Fig. 30

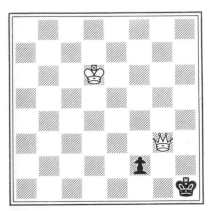

Fig. 30a

Fig. 30 gives an example of such play:

1.	Qe7+	Kf1
2.	Qd6	Ke2
3.	Qe5+	Kf2
4.	Qd4+	Ke2
5.	Qe4+	Kf2
6.	Qd3	Ke1
7.	Qe3+	Kd1
8.	Kd7	Kc2
9.	Qe2	Kc1
10.	Qc4+	Kb2
11.	Qd3	Kc1

[32]

12.	Qc3+	Kd1
13.	Kd6	

and so on until the White King reaches the square d3 and a winning position.

In the case of the exceptions mentioned, it will be seen from Fig. 30a that if the White Queen takes the pawn on f2 the Black King will be stalemated and the game is therefore a draw as the pawn cannot be successfully taken.

King, Rook and pawn Endings

The following general statements apply to endings involving King and Rook against King, Rook and pawn:

1. If the opposing King is in front of the pawn, a draw can be obtained.
2. If the opposing King is cut off from the pawn by two files or more he will lose, except perhaps in case of a pawn very far back.
3. If the opposing King is cut off by one file only, he can draw if he is in the smaller half of the board, but can lose if he is in the larger.

Fig. 31 shows the King in front of the pawn and after:

1. e5 Ra6;
2. e6 Ra1

it is clear that Black can draw the game by perpetual check from behind or else he will win the pawn and secure a draw in that way.

If the King is cut off from the pawn by two files or more as in Fig. 31a, the plan for White is to get his King in front of his pawn on the eighth rank

Fig. 31

Fig. 31a

and then to bring it out again so as to block the check from the Black Rook at the appropriate moment.

1. Kf5   Rb6
2. e6   Rb1
3. Kf6   Rf1+
4. Ke7   Re1
5. Kf7   Rf1+
6. Ke8   Re1
7. e7   Rd1
8. Rg4   Rd2
9. Kf7   Rf2+
10. Ke6   Re2+
11. Kf6   Rf2+
12. Ke5   Re2+
13. Re4 and wins

Fig. 31b shows the position when the King is cut off by one file in the smaller section of the board. Black can draw this game and it is clear that after:

1. Kd5   Ra5+

the game is a draw by perpetual check or the loss of the White pawn, since if the White King takes shelter on the f file, Black immediately plays his King across in front of the pawn and secures a draw as in Fig. 31.

·In Fig. 31c the King is cut off by one

Fig. 31b

Fig. 31c

file in the larger half of the board and will lose after:

1. Rh4+
2. Kf5 Rh5+
3. Kf6 Rh6+
4. Kg5

and the White pawn must now reach e6 and eventually e8 and win.

In many of the examples quoted, statements have been made, as in the explanation of Fig. 31c, that the White pawn must now be able to get to e8, or that White now wins. It will be excellent practice for the beginner to work out the truth of such statements for himself because they are not always obvious except to more experienced players, and in working them out, the player will gradually learn more of the game.

Game Openings

Some basic principles and examples have been given of the start, the middle and the end of a game of chess and finally there are now given, without any comments, a few examples of some of the more usual openings used in club games. These are intended to give the beginner some sort of picture of how a game starts, but the theory of opening play is so immense that nothing more can be attempted here.

King's pawn Openings

Ruy Lopez

1.	e4	e5	
2.	Nf3	Nc6	
3.	Bb5	a6	
4.	Ba4	d6 . . . or	. . . Nf6
5.	B×c6+	b×c6	O–O Be7
6.	d4	f6	Re1 b5

Giuoco Piano

1.	e4	e5
2.	Nf3	Nc6
3.	Bc4	Bc5
4.	c3	Nf6
5.	d4	e×d4
6.	c×d4	Bb4+

French Defence

1.	e4	e6
2.	d4	d5
3.	Nc3	Nf6
4.	Bg5	Be7
5.	e5	Nfd7
6.	B×e7	Qxe7

Caro-Kann Defence

1.	e4	c6
2.	d4	d5
3.	Nc3	d×e4
4.	N×e4	Bf5
5.	Ng3	Bg6

Sicilian Defence

1.	e4	c5		
2.	Nf3	Nc6	or Nc3	Nc6
3.	d4	c×d4	g3	g6
4.	Nxd4	Nf6	Bg2	Bg7
5.	Nc3	d6	d3	e6

Queen's pawn Openings

Queen's Gambit

	Accepted		Declined	
1.	d4	d5	d4	d5
2.	c4	d×c4	c4	e6
3.	Nf3	Nf6	Nc3	Nf6
4.	e3	e6	Bg5	Be7
5.	B×c4	c5	e3	O–O
6.	O–O	a6	Nf3	h6
7.	Qe2	Nc6	Bh4	Ne4

King's Indian Defence

1. d4   Nf6
2. c4   g6
3. Nc3   Bg7
4. e4   d6
5. Nf3   O–O
6. Be2   Nbd7
7. O–O   e5

Nimzo-Indian Defence

1. d4   Nf6
2. c4   e6
3. Nc3   Bb4
4. a3   B×c3+
5. b×c3 c5
6. e3   O–O

The examples given represent openings that are frequently used in chess, but there are, of course, many different variations of each of the systems illustrated and also very many other types of openings altogether. They all represent, however, attempts to carry out the same basic principles of opening play as indicated earlier in this book, and it may be of interest to the beginner to note how these principles are applied in the examples given.

Conclusion

This book constitutes a very brief attempt to cover the enormous subject of 'how to play chess', but if the novice works through the examples carefully with a set and board in front of him he will begin to absorb the fascination of this, the finest indoor game in the world. His course thereafter is clear; to join a chess club and to develop his play by constant practice and the tuition of more experienced members. The main school of chess, however, is experience and nothing but playing hard and often will really make a player.

Chess clubs do not always advertise themselves as well as they might, but the British Chess Federation will be pleased to tell the novice his nearest club or direct him to a local organiser who will know.

Subscribing to a good chess magazine will also help the novice, and the BCF will send a list on receipt of a s.a.e. Amongst these is the **British Chess Magazine**, owned by the BCF, and a specimen copy can be sent on request.

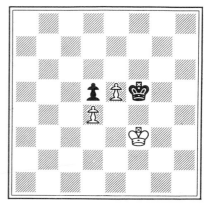

Study 1   White to play and win.

Study 2   White to play and win.

Study 3 White to play and Black to win.

Study 4 White to play and win.

The BCF will also be pleased to help with all other kinds of enquiries about the game. Write to:

**The British Chess Federation
9a Grand Parade
ST LEONARDS-ON-SEA
East Sussex
TN38 ODD**

Studies (pawn endings)

Solutions

1. The technique is for the White King to go to the other side when the Black King cannot keep him out, e.g. 1. Ke3 Ke6; 2. Kd3 Kd7; 3. Kc3 Kc6; 4. Kb4 Kb6; 5. Ka4! (this is the point of the manoeuvre. Black cannot now oppose the White King by . . . Ka6 because of e6!) . . . Kc6; 6. Ka5 Kc7; 7. Kb5 Kd7; 8. Kc5 Ke6; 9. Kc6 and the Black pawn is now lost.

2. White gains his objective by moving his King along the lines of a triangle, e.g. 1. Kd5 Kc8; 2. Kd4 Kd8; (if. . . . Kc7; then Kc5 as in the text) 3. Kc4 Kc8; 4. Kd5 — the move which forces Black to give up the opposition — Kc7 (forced otherwise Kd6 wins): 5. Kc5 Kc8; 6. Kb6 Kb8; 7. K×a6 Kc7; 8. Kb5 Kc8; 9. Kb6 Kb8; 10. c7+ Kc8; 11. a6 Kd7; 12. Kb7 and wins.

3. Here White is in a position to stop the Black Pawn from queening; but he cannot maintain his King in this commanding position, e.g. 1. d4 Kb7; 2. d5 Kc7; 3. K moves and Black wins with a2.

4. Black allowed White to exchange Queens on g7 thinking his passed h-pawns would win but could not overcome White's stunning move 1. e5! If he had taken, 2. c5 Kf8 3. c6 and the White a-pawn would have queened. 1. . . . Kf8; 2. e×d6 Ke8; 3. Kg3 Kd7; 4. c5 Kc6(a); 5. Kh4 and wins. White won because he could force Black to 'give' him self-supporting pawns.
   (a) Black must prevent c6: so his King can only be on d7 or c6.

In all Studies White plays from bottom of board.